LAUGH OUT LOUD!
THE OUT TO SEA
JOKE BOOK

Sean Connolly

WINDMILL BOOKS

New York

Published in 2013 by Windmill Books, An Imprint of Rosen Publishing
29 East 21st Street, New York, NY 10010

First Edition

Editor: Joe Harris
Illustrations: Adam Clay (cover) and Dynamo Design (interiors)
Layout Design: Notion Design

Library of Congress Cataloging-in-Publication Data

Connolly, Sean, 1956–
 The out to sea joke book / by Sean Connolly. — 1st ed.
    p. cm. — (Laugh out loud)
Includes index.
ISBN 978-1-61533-647-0 (library binding) — ISBN 978-1-61533-660-9 (pbk.) —
ISBN 978-1-61533-661-6 (6-pack)
1. Ocean travel—Humor. 2. Riddles, Juvenile. I. Title.
PN6231.O27C55 2013
808.88'2—dc23
                                    2012019523

Printed in China

CPSIA Compliance Information: Batch #AW3102WM: For Further Information contact Windmill Books, New York, New York at 1-866-478-0556
SL002424US

CONTENTS

Jokes.................................... 4

Glossary................................. 32

Index.................................... 32

Further Reading.......................... 32

Websites................................. 32

OUT TO SEA

Teacher: Who can tell me which sea creature eats its prey two at a time?
Pupil: Noah's shark!

What do sea captains tell their children at night?
Ferry tales.

Where do fish sleep?
On a waterbed!

Teacher: What musical instrument do Spanish fishermen play?
Cast-a-nets!

Why don't clams give to charity?
Because they're shellfish.

PLEASE GIVE GENEROUSLY

Teacher: Why was no one able to play cards on Noah's Ark?
Pupil: Because Noah stood on the deck!

What kind of noise makes an oyster grouchy?
A noisy noise annoys an oyster!

Teacher: Where do you find starfish?
Pupil: In the Galack Sea!

Teacher: Why have you brought that fish into school?
Pupil: Because we will be practicing scales in the music lesson!

Which beach item gets wetter the more it dries?
A towel.

What lies at the bottom of the ocean and shakes?
A nervous wreck.

Customer: Waiter, what's wrong with this fish?
Waiter: Long time, no sea.

What happened when the restless sleeper bought himself a waterbed?
He got seasick.

Lifeguard: You can't fish on this stretch of beach!
Boy with fishing rod: I'm not—I'm teaching my pet worm to swim.

What happened when the salmon went to Hollywood?
He became a starfish.

Why don't fish parents tell their children about electric eels?
They're just too shocking.

What music do they play in underwater nightclubs?
Sole music!

What did the passing seagull say to the pilot of the motorboat with no engine?
"How's it going?"

Which television show is the most popular with fish?
Name That Tuna.

Which two fish can you wear on your feet?
A sole and an eel.

Did you hear about the two fish in a tank?
One was driving, and the other was manning the guns.

Wife: Doctor, is there any hope for my husband? He thinks he's a shipwreck.
Doctor: I'm afraid he's sunk, ma'am.

Why did the man go swimming in his best clothes?
He thought he needed a wet suit.

How do jellyfish police capture criminals?
In sting operations.

What did the walrus do after he read the sad book?
He started to blubber.

How can you
tell that the
ocean is feeling
friendly?
It keeps waving
at you.

Which fish once
ruled Russia?
The tsar-dine.

How can you tell two octopuses are dating?
Because they walk along arm in arm in arm in arm in arm
in arm in arm in arm!

What can you expect from a clever crab?
Snappy answers!

How could you give yourself an injury gathering shellfish?
You might pull a mussel.

How do fish go into business?
They start on a small scale.

What was the shark's favorite book?
Huckleberry Fin.

Where can you find an ocean with no water?
On a map.

Why was the little iceberg just like his dad?
Because he was a chip off the cold block.

Why do whales sing?
Because they can't talk!

What do you call a gull that flies over a bay?
A bay-gull.

OUT TO SEA

Why did the scuba diver hear underwater singing?
He was in the Coral Sea.

How do you keep in touch with a fish?
You drop it a line.

What is the coldest animal in the sea?
The blue whale.

Did you hear about the fisherman and the shepherd?
They got along by hook or by crook.

Why did Captain Hook cross the road?
To get to the second-hand store.

OUT TO SEA

What day do fish hate?
Fry day.

Where do ocean scientists keep their coffee mugs?
On the continental shelf.

Where do fish keep their savings?
In the river bank!

What do you call a man floating up and down on the sea?
Bob.

What happened when the boat carrying red paint crashed into one carrying blue paint?
Both crews were marooned.

Who stole the soap from the bathtub?
A robber duckie.

Why are dolphins smarter than humans?
Because they can train humans to stand by the side of the pool and throw them fish.

What is the fight song of the pig navy?
"Oinkers Aweigh."

Why didn't the sea captain's radio work in rough seas?
It was on the wrong wavelength.

What kind of fish are useful in cold weather?
Skates.

Why did the ship's captain look fed up? He had a sinking feeling.

Why don't traffic lights ever go swimming? They take too long to change.

Which sea creatures are the biggest cry babies?
Whales.

What sort of hair style do mermaids have?
Wavy.

What did Santa say when he first spotted America?
"Land ho, ho, ho!"

How does an octopus go to war?
Well-armed.

Do undersea creatures play baseball?
Yes—there are 20,000 leagues under the sea.

What do pigs wear when they go swimming?
Hoggles.

What's black, incredibly rude, and
floats on water?
Crude oil.

What is a pirate's
favorite movie?
Booty and the Beast.

OUT TO SEA

What do British sea monsters eat?
Fish and ships!

What's fluffy and green?
A seasick poodle.

Why did the crab cross the road?
To get to the other tide.

Where is the safest place to see a man-eating fish?
In a seafood restaurant.

What grades did the pirate get in school?
High seas.

Which salad
ingredient is
the most
dangerous for
ocean liners?
Iceberg lettuce.

Who held the baby octopus for ransom?
Squidnappers!

What's the best medicine for seasickness?
Vitamin sea.

What do you get if you cross a bad golfer and an outboard
motor?
I'm not sure, but I bet it goes, "Putt, putt, putt, putt."

Which fish come out at night?
Starfish.

Who wins all the money at the undersea poker games?
Card sharks.

What happens if you cross an electric eel with a sponge?
You get a shock absorber.

Why do pirates have a hard time learning the alphabet?
Because they spend so long at "C."

How can fishermen save on gas?
By carp-pooling.

How do you close an envelope underwater?
With a seal.

OUT TO SEA

What runs and runs without ever getting out of breath?
A river.

What do the underwater police travel in?
Squid cars!

What sort of snacks can you buy on a Chinese boat?
Junk food!

How did Robinson Crusoe survive after his ship sank?
He found some soap and washed himself ashore.

Why wouldn't the sailor eat any fruitcake?
He was worried about dangerous currants.

OUT TO SEA

What sort of boats do clever schoolchildren travel on?
Scholar-ships!

What are pirates' favorite vegetables?
Aaaaartichokes.

What did the deep-sea diver yell when he got caught in seaweed?
"Kelp!"

What do you get if you meet a shark in the Arctic Ocean?
Frostbite.

What did Cinderella wear when she went skin-diving?
Glass flippers.

Which sea
creature can also fly?
A pilot whale.

Why did the pirate go into the computer store?
To buy an iPatch.

Why are goldfish orange?
The water makes them rusty.

Why did the surfer wear a baseball glove?
Because he wanted to catch a wave.

What do you call a delinquent octopus?
A crazy, mixed-up squid!

Why did the sailor jump rope?
He was the ship's skipper.

What do sailors paint with?
Watercolors.

What did the ship say as it sailed into the harbor?
"What's up, dock?"

Why do fish in a school all swim in the same direction?
They're playing Salmon Says.

Are shellfish warm to touch?
No, they feel clammy.

Are sharks fat?
No, they're just fin and bones.

What did the shark plead in the murder case?
Not gill-ty.

How did the fisherman become rich?
He increased his net profits.

What did the pirate say when he got his wooden leg
caught in a freezer?
"Shiver me timbers."

What is the Loch Ness
Monster's favorite meal?
A submarine sandwich.

What is in the middle of a jellyfish?
A jellybutton.

Where would you find a down-and-out octopus?
On squid row.

What do whales like to chew?
Blubber gum.

How do fish get to school?
By octobus.

Why did the burglar
buy a surfboard?
He wanted to
start a crime
wave!

Who is the
ocean's most
dangerous outlaw?
Billy the Squid.

Where do mermaids go to see movies?
The dive-in.

What did the fisherman say to the magician?
"Pick a cod, any cod."

How much sand would be in a hole two feet long, two feet
wide, and two feet deep?
None—holes are empty!

What grouchy animal lives on the beach and ignores
its neighbors?
A hermit crab.

Which fish works in a hospital?
A plastic sturgeon.

What's the best way to stuff a lobster?
Take it out for pizza and ice cream.

What do you call a baby squid?
A little squirt.

What position does the crab play on the baseball team?
He's the pinch hitter.

How is it that after a ship sank and every single person died, there were two people left?
They were married.

OUT TO SEA

How do you get a car unstuck in a mudflat?
With four-eel drive.

What happened when the tuna fisherman was caught stealing?
He got canned.

What happens to a green rock when you throw it into the Red Sea?
It gets wet.

What do you get when you graduate from scuba diving school?
A deep-loma.

What do you call a massive mallard?
Moby Duck.

OUT TO SEA

What do you get when you cross a bee with a seagull?
A beagle.

How does a penguin feel when it is left all alone?
Ice-olated.

What can you put into a barrel full of water to make it lighter?
A hole.

What do pirates use as kindling?
Fish sticks.

Why do sea lions swim in salt water?
Because pepper makes them sneeze.

OUT TO SEA

Which fish go to
heaven when they
die?
Angelfish.

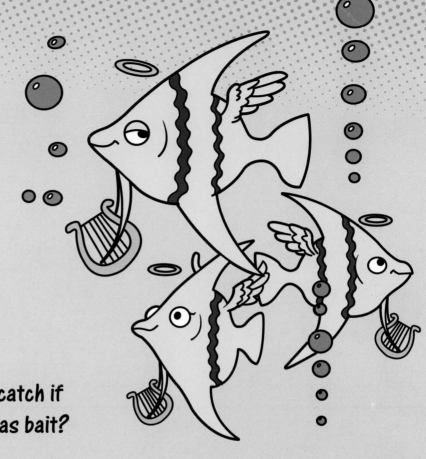

Why did the bargain
hunters turn up at
the harbor?
They had heard
about the sails.

What are you likely to catch if
you use peanut butter as bait?
Jellyfish.

I'm on a seafood diet.
Are you losing weight?
No, because every time I see food, I eat it.

How did the dolphin make decisions?
It would flipper coin.

OUT TO SEA

Who is the head of the underwater Mafia?
The codfather.

What kind of fish likes to eat between meals?
A snackerel.

What game do fish like to play at parties?
Tide and seek.

What did the pirate say to the woman in the shoe store?
"Where's my booties?"

What is a knight's favorite fish?
A swordfish.

OUT TO SEA

How does a boat show affection?
It hugs the shore.

How do lighthouse keepers communicate with each other?
With shine language.

What can fly underwater?
A mosquito in a submarine.

What do you use to cut the ocean in half?
A seasaw.

Which fish are the best at home-improvement projects?
Hammerhead sharks.

Glossary

delinquent (dih-LING-kwent)
a young person who breaks
the law

loch (LOK) a lake in Scotland

maroon (muh-ROON) a deep,
reddish-purple color

scuba diving (SKOO-buh DY-ving)
diving underwater with a tank
of air and flippers

sturgeon (STER-jin) a large,
bony fish

Further Reading

Jacobs, Pat. *I Wonder Why Pirates Wore Earrings and Other Questions About Pirates.* New York: Kingfisher, 2012.

Lewman, David. *Yo-Ho-Ha-Ha-Ha!* New York: Simon Spotlight, 2007.

Taylor, Barbara. *Viewfinder: Oceans.* San Diego, CA: Silver Dolphin Books, 2011.

Index

crabs 9, 16, 25, 26
dolphins 13, 29
icebergs 10, 17
jellyfish 8, 24, 29
Noah 4, 5
octopuses 9, 15, 17, 21, 24
penguins 28
pirates 15, 16, 18, 20, 21, 23, 28, 30
sailors 19, 22
sharks 4, 10, 18, 20, 23, 31
squid 17, 19, 21, 24, 25, 26
submarines 23, 31
whales 10, 11, 14, 21, 24

Websites

For Web resources related to the subject of this book, go to: www.windmillbooks.com/weblinks and select this book's title.